I Spy
CHRISTMAS

Alek Malkovich

I SPY with my little eye, something beginning with...

A is for

Angel

I SPY with my little eye, something beginning with...

B

is for

Bell

I SPY with my little eye, something beginning with...

C and D

C is for

Candy cane

D is for

Decorations

I SPY with my little eye, something beginning with...

E  is for

Elf

I SPY with my little eye, something beginning with...

F

is for

Fruit cake

I SPY with my little eye, something beginning with...

G and H

G is for

Gingerbread

H is for

Holly

I SPY with my little eye, something beginning with...

I is for

Ice skates

I SPY with my little eye, something beginning with...

J is for

Jack frost

I SPY with my little eye, something beginning with...

K and L

K is for

Kris Kringle

L is for
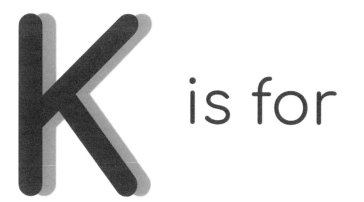

Lights

I SPY with my little eye, something beginning with...

M is for

Mittens

I SPY with my little eye, something beginning with...

N  is for

Nutcracker

I SPY with my little eye, something beginning with...

O and P

O is for

Orange peel

P is for

Presents

I SPY with my little eye, something beginning with...

 **Q** is for

Quince jelly

I SPY with my little eye, something beginning with...

R is for

Rudolf

I SPY with my little eye, something beginning with...

S and T

S is for Snowman

T is for Train

I SPY with my little eye, something beginning with...

U is for

Ugly sweater

I SPY with my little eye, something beginning with...

V is for

Vixen

I SPY with my little eye, something beginning with...

W and X

W is for

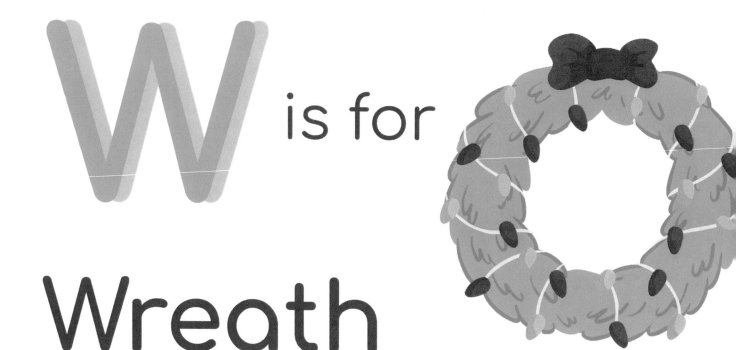

Wreath

X is for

Xmas

I SPY with my little eye, something beginning with...

Y is for

Yule log cake

I SPY with my little eye, something beginning with...

Z is for

Zebra

Made in the USA
Columbia, SC
22 October 2021